Easy Main Dishes
From Around the World

Heather Alexander

Enslow Elementary

Library of Congress Cataloging-in-Publication Data

Alexander, Heather, 1967-
  Easy main dishes from around the world / Heather Alexander.
      p. cm. — (Easy cookbooks for kids)
  Includes index.
  Summary: "Learn how to make eleven main dishes from around the world, such as swedish meatballs, jollof rice, papaya chicken and coconut milk, and sweet and sour shrimp"—Provided by publisher.
      ISBN 978-0-7660-3766-3
  1. Entrées (Cooking)—Juvenile literature. 2. Cooking (Meat)—Juvenile literature. 3. International cooking–Juvenile literature. 4. Quick and easy cooking—Juvenile literature. 5. Cookbooks. I. Title.
  TX740.A44 2011
  641.5'55—dc22
                                    2010046429

Paperback ISBN 978-1-59845-273-0

Printed in China

052011 Leo Paper Group, Heshan City, Guangdong, China

10 9 8 7 6 5 4 3 2 1

To Our Readers: We have done our best to make sure all Internet Addresses in this book were active and appropriate when we went to press. However, the author and the publisher have no control over and assume no liability for the material available on those Internet sites or on other Web sites they may link to. Any comments or suggestions can be sent by e-mail to comments@enslow.com or to the address on the back cover.

Every effort has been made to locate all copyright holders of material used in this book. If any errors or omissions have occurred, corrections will be made in future editions of this book.

Warning: The recipes in this book contain ingredients to which people may be allergi... such as peanuts and milk.

Contents

Introduction: Time to Cook!

Have you ever met a kid from another country? Maybe you've seen photos or movies of kids from around the world. They probably seem very different from you. They may speak a different language, wear different clothes, or live in a different kind of house. But no matter what part of the world kids live in, they all get hungry and they all like to eat a delicious dinner. Even though dinner seems like a big meal, there are many easy dishes that you can cook that will have your family asking for seconds.

Food brings the world together. It tells a story about each country. Food can tell you about how people live as well as about the climate, the history, and the ingredients that are grown in each country. Cooking—and eating—are a fun and yummy way to learn about other cultures.

So tie on an apron and let's cook easy main courses from all over the world.

Be Safe!

Whenever you are in the kitchen, there are important safety rules to follow.

1. Always **ask a responsible adult** for permission to cook. Always **have an adult** by your side when you use the oven, the stove, knives, or any appliance.

2. If you have long hair, tie it back. Remove dangling jewelry and tuck in any loose clothing.

3. Always use pot holders or oven mitts when handling anything on the stove or in the oven.

4. Never rush while cutting ingredients. You don't want the knife to slip.

5. If you are cooking something in the oven, stay in the house. Always use a timer—and stay where you can hear it.

6. If you are cooking something on the stove, stay in the kitchen.

7. ALLERGY ALERT! If you are cooking for someone else, let him or her know what ingredients you are using. Some people have life-threatening allergies to such foods as peanuts and shellfish.

Cooking Tips and Tricks

Keeping Clean:

- Wash your hands before you start. Make sure to also wash your hands after touching raw poultry, meat, or seafood and after cracking eggs. These ingredients may have harmful germs that can make you very sick. Wash knives and cutting boards well with soap and water after they've touched these ingredients.

- Rinse all fruits and vegetables under cool water before you use them.

- Make sure your work space is clean before you start.

- Clean up as you cook.

Planning Ahead:

- Read the recipe from beginning to end before you start cooking. Make sure you have all the ingredients and tools you will need before you start.

- If you don't understand something in a recipe, ask an adult for help.

Measuring:

- To measure dry ingredients, such as flour and sugar, dip the correct size measuring cup into the ingredient until it is full. Then level off the top of the cup with the flat side of a butter knife. Brown sugar is the only dry ingredient that should be tightly packed into a measuring cup.

- To measure the liquid ingredients, such as oil and milk, use a clear glass or plastic measuring cup. Make sure it is on a flat surface. Pour the liquid into the cup until it reaches the correct level. Check the measurement at eye level.

- Keep in mind that measuring spoons come in different sizes. Be sure you are using a *teaspoon* if the recipe asks for it and not a *tablespoon*.

Mixing:

- Beat—Mix ingredients together *fast* with a wooden spoon, a whisk, or an electric mixer.

- Mix—Blend ingredients together with a wooden spoon, an electric mixer, or a whisk.

- Stir—Combine ingredients together with a wooden or metal spoon.

Cooking Basics:

- Cooling food—After food has been baked in the oven, place it on a wire rack until it is no longer hot.

- Cracking an egg—Hold the egg in one hand. Crack the eggshell against the side of a bowl. Using both hands, pull the eggshell apart over the bowl so the yolk and the white drop into the bowl.

- Juicing—To get the juice from a lemon, lime, or orange, cut the fruit in half and press it against the top of a juicer until all the juice is out. The juicer will strain out the seeds and leave you with the juice. For most recipes, you can use ready-made juice instead.

- Preheating—Turn the oven on at least 15 minutes before you need to use it.

Cooking Terms

Cooking has its own vocabulary. Here are some terms you should be familiar with:

bread (verb)—To coat with breadcrumbs or flour before frying.

chop (verb)—To cut into bite-sized pieces.

dice (verb)—To cut into small pieces (smaller than chopped).

drizzle (verb)—To pour a small amount of liquid in a stream over a dish.

mince (verb)—To cut into very small pieces.

sauté (verb)—To cook quickly in a pan over high heat using a small amount of oil or butter, stirring all the time.

shred (verb)—To tear into small pieces.

simmer (verb)—To boil slowly at a low temperature.

Cooking Tools

baking dish

cutting board

cookie sheet

colander

frying pan

juicer

electric mixer

measuring cups

oven mitt

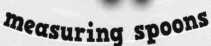

measuring spoons

sauce pan

pie pan

potato masher

paring knife

rolling pin

tongs

wooden spoon

slotted spoon

spatula

whisk

wok

vegetable peeler

Nutrition

The best food is healthy as well as delicious. In planning meals, keep in mind the guidelines of the food pyramid.

GRAINS	VEGETABLES	FRUITS	MILK	MEAT & BEANS
Make half your grains whole	Vary your veggies	Focus on fruits	Get your calcium-rich foods	Go lean with protein
Eat at least 3 oz. of whole-grain cereals, breads, crackers, rice, or pasta every day 1 oz. is about 1 slice of bread, about 1 cup of breakfast cereal, or ½ cup of cooked rice, cereal, or pasta	Eat more dark-green veggies like broccoli, spinach, and other dark leafy greens Eat more orange vegetables like carrots and sweet potatoes Eat more dry beans and peas like pinto beans, kidney beans, and lentils	Eat a variety of fruit Choose fresh, frozen, canned, or dried fruit Go easy on fruit juices	Go low-fat or fat-free when you choose milk, yogurt, and other milk products If you don't or can't consume milk, choose lactose-free products or other calcium sources such as fortified foods and beverages	Choose low-fat or lean meats and poultry Bake it, broil it, or grill it Vary your protein routine — choose more fish, beans, peas, nuts, and seeds

For a 2,000-calorie diet, you need the amounts below from each food group. To find the amounts that are right for you, go to MyPyramid.gov.

GRAINS	VEGETABLES	FRUITS	MILK	MEAT & BEANS
Eat 6 oz. every day	Eat 2½ cups every day	Eat 2 cups every day	Get 3 cups every day; for kids aged 2 to 8, it's 2	Eat 5½ oz. every day

Conversions

Recipes list amounts needed. Sometimes you need to know what that amount equals in another measurement. And sometimes you may want to make twice as much (or half as much) as the recipe yields. This chart will help you.

DRY INGREDIENT MEASUREMENTS	
Measure	**Equivalent**
1 tablespoon	3 teaspoons
¼ cup	4 tablespoons
½ cup	8 tablespoons
1 cup	16 tablespoons
2 cups	1 pound
½ stick of butter	¼ cup
1 stick of butter	½ cup
2 sticks of butter	1 cup
LIQUID INGREDIENT MEASUREMENTS	
8 fluid ounces	1 cup
1 pint (16 ounces)	2 cups
1 quart (2 pints)	4 cups
1 gallon (4 quarts)	16 cups

This book does not use abbreviations for measurements, but many cookbooks do. Here's what they mean:

c—cup

oz.—ounce

lb.—pound

T or tbsp.—tablespoon

t or tsp.—teaspoon

Chapter 1

Köttbollar

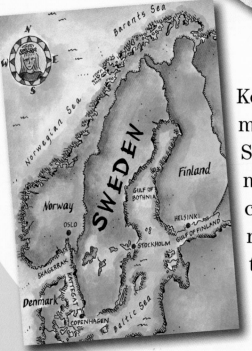

Köttbollar (*shut-bullahr*), or Swedish meatballs, are the national dish of Sweden. They are smaller than Italian meatballs and are served with a cream sauce and potatoes or buttered noodles. A spice called nutmeg gives the meatballs their sweet taste.

Sweden

Sweden is in northern Europe and is part of an area called Scandinavia, which also includes Denmark and Norway. More than half the country is covered by thick forests. Red lingonberries (*LING-gun berries*) grow in the Swedish forests, and the meatballs are often eaten with tart lingonberry jam.

What You Need

Equipment:
Large mixing bowl
Large frying pan
Slotted spoon
Oven-safe dish
Whisk

Ingredients:
<u>For meatballs:</u>
2 pounds ground beef or 1 pound ground beef and 1 pound ground pork or veal
1 cup bread crumbs
1 egg, beaten
¼ cup milk
½ cup onion, diced
½ teaspoon salt
¼ teaspoon pepper
½ teaspoon nutmeg
¼ teaspoon allspice
3 tablespoons butter

<u>For gravy:</u>
¼ cup all-purpose flour
2 cups beef broth
¼ cup heavy or sour cream

<u>For sauteing:</u>
2 tablespoons vegetable oil

What's This?

The name "allspice" may sound like it is a blend of other spices, but it's not. Allspice is sometimes called "Jamaica pepper."

Let's Cook!

1. Preheat oven to 200°F (93°C).

2. In a large bowl, combine all the meatball ingredients. Using clean hands, shape the meat into about 36 meatballs about the size of Ping-Pong balls.

3. Heat two tablespoons of vegetable oil over medium heat in a large frying pan. Add the meatballs in two batches. Cook the meatballs, turning with a slotted spoon, until they are golden brown on all sides (about 7–10 minutes).

4. Using the slotted spoon, place the meatballs in an oven-safe dish and place the dish in the warm oven. Repeat with the remaining meatballs.

5. Make the gravy by adding flour to the frying pan and turning the heat down to low. Whisk about 1 minute and then add beef broth and cream. Whisk about 5 minutes until gravy thickens.

6. Add the meatballs to the gravy and stir gently until covered. Serve warm with noodles or potatoes. You may want to use toothpicks to eat the meatballs.

Makes 4–6 servings, or about 36 meatballs.

Cook's Tip

Wet your hands with cold water before shaping the meatballs so the meat doesn't stick to your hands.

Did You Know?

Swedish meatballs are part of smorgasbords (SMORE-gus-boards) in Sweden. A smorgasbord is an all-you-can-eat buffet.

Chapter 2

Sweet and Sour Shrimp

Sweet and sour shrimp is a meal from China. The dish combines two different flavors for a tangy taste. The dish has what is called "the yin and yang of Chinese cooking." The phrase means that everything is in balance or in harmony. The sweet taste does not overpower the sour taste, and the sour does not overpower the sweet taste.

China

China is a huge country in eastern Asia. More than one billion people live in China. Sweet and sour sauce comes from the Cantonese region, which is in the eastern part of the country and includes the city of Hong Kong.

How to Use Chopsticks

In China people use chopsticks instead of a fork and knife.

1. Place the upper chopstick between the tips of your index and middle fingers and hold it with your thumb, just like you hold a pencil.

2. Place the bottom chopstick in the crook of your thumb with the middle of the chopstick resting on your ring finger.

3. Move the upper chopstick by bending your thumb and index finger. Keep the bottom chopstick still. Have the tips of the chopsticks come together like claws to pick up the food.

What You Need

Equipment:

1 medium bowl

1 small bowl

Wok or stir-fry pan

Slotted spoon

Plate

Ingredients:

1 tablespoon soy sauce

1 teaspoon cornstarch

1 pound medium shrimp, peeled and deveined with tails cut off

1 tablespoon vegetable oil

1 bell pepper (green or red), diced

1 small onion, thinly sliced

2 teaspoons ginger, minced

2 teaspoons garlic, minced

1 16-ounce can pineapple chunks

Cook's Tip

To devein shrimp, have an adult use a paring knife to cut along the back of the shrimp and pull out the black vein.

Sauce:

2 tablespoons cornstarch

2 tablespoons soy sauce

1 tablespoon rice vinegar

2 tablespoons ketchup

3 tablespoons sugar

2 tablespoons orange juice

Cook's Tip

To mince garlic, separate the cloves from the head of the garlic, peel off the skin from each clove, and then chop into tiny pieces.

Let's Cook!

1. Combine 1 tablespoon soy sauce and 1 teaspoon cornstarch in a medium bowl. Put in the shrimp and marinate, or soak, for 10 minutes.

2. In a small bowl, mix together all the sauce ingredients. Set aside.

3. Heat a wok or stir-fry pan over medium-high heat. Add oil to coat pan. Add shrimp and cook about 2 minutes until pink.

4. Remove shrimp from pan with a slotted spoon and place on a plate.

5. Add pepper, onion, ginger, and garlic, to the pan and cook on medium heat for 2 minutes. Then add sauce and stir until sauce thickens.

6. Return shrimp to the pan. Add pineapple. Mix well.

7. Serve hot over rice.

Makes 4–6 servings.

What's This?

Rice vinegar is clear vinegar from China or Japan. It can be found in the Asian food aisle in your market.

Cook's Tip

While you're cooking, place shrimp in a bowl of ice water to keep them fresh.

Chapter 3

Jollof Rice

Jollof (*JAH-luff*) rice is from the West African countries of Nigeria, Senegal, and Gambia. It is a hearty dish made with rice, tomatoes, and usually chicken. Jollof rice can be made many different ways with any kind of meat, fish, or vegetable.

West Africa

Most meals in West Africa are cooked in one pot. The weather is hot in West Africa, because all the countries are near the equator, but the people like their food even hotter, or spicier. When West Africans were taken to America as slaves hundreds of years ago, they brought their food with them. "Red rice" jambalaya (*jahm-buh-LIE-uh*) from Louisiana is very similar to jollof rice.

What You Need

Equipment:

Large skillet with lid or
Dutch oven
Slotted spoon
Knife
Cutting board

What's This?

A Dutch oven is a
thick metal pot with a
tight-fitting cover.

Cook's Tip

You can use either leftover
chicken or prepackaged, cooked
chicken that is already cut up.

Ingredients:

2 tablespoons vegetable oil

1½ pounds chicken cut into
large cubes

1 onion, diced

3 cloves garlic, minced

1 large tomato, diced

1½ cups chicken broth

1 6-ounce can tomato paste

½ teaspoon dried thyme
(*time*)

¼ teaspoon black pepper

1 cup long-grain rice

1 cup water

¼ teaspoon salt

Optional assorted washed,
peeled, and chopped
vegetables (green beans,
carrots, bell peppers,
and/or mushrooms)

⅛ teaspoon crushed red
pepper flakes (optional)

21

Let's Cook!

1. In a large skillet or Dutch oven, heat oil and cook chicken until brown on the outside and no longer pink on the inside. Using a slotted spoon, carefully remove chicken from the pan and place on a plate.

2. To the remaining oil in the pan, add the onion and garlic and cook about 5 minutes until golden.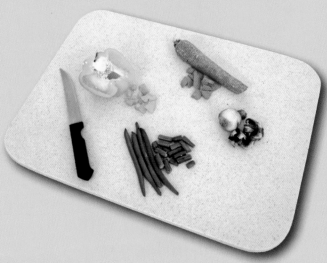

3. Add chicken broth, tomato paste, thyme, pepper, salt, vegetables, and cooked chicken pieces to the pan and simmer for 5 minutes.

4. Add rice and water. Bring to a boil and then reduce heat and cover. Simmer on low for 30 minutes. Stir occasionally.

5. Remove pan from heat and let stand for 10 minutes. Spoon jollof onto a serving platter. Spinkle crushed red pepper flakes to taste.

Makes 4–6 servings.

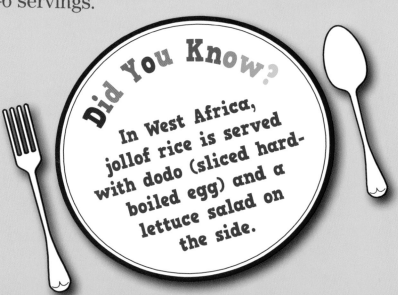

Did You Know?

In West Africa, jollof rice is served with dodo (sliced hard-boiled egg) and a lettuce salad on the side.

Spaghetti al Pomodoro e Basilico

(Spaghetti with Tomatoes and Basil)

Pasta is eaten every day in Italy. In fact, Italians eat an average of fifty-five pounds of pasta a year each!

Spaghetti is long, thin pasta that in Italian means "little strings." This dish, spaghetti al pomodoro e basilico (*ol poh-mo-DOOR-oh ay bah-SEE-lee-coh*), it is served with a fresh tomato sauce flavored with basil.

Italy

Italy, a country in southern Europe, is shaped something like a boot. Naples, in southern Italy, is the center of pasta making. Pasta dough is made from wheat. It is shaped, cut, and then dried. There are many shapes of pasta, and this recipe can be made with any of them.

23

How to Eat Spaghetti

Italians never cut spaghetti with a knife and fork. Instead they twirl the spaghetti around their fork. Here's how:

1. Take a little bunch of the spaghetti with the prongs of your fork. Push it against your spoon or the side of your bowl.
2. Twirl your fork clockwise to roll the spaghetti around it so all the strands are tucked in.
3. Raise the fork with the spaghetti wrapped around it and eat. Enjoy!

What You Need

Equipment:

Large pot
Frying pan
Large spoon
Colander
Serving dish

Ingredients:

2 pounds fresh ripe tomatoes
2 tablespoons olive oil
½ cup chopped onion
3 cloves garlic, peeled and chopped
15–20 basil leaves, shredded
1 pound spaghetti
¾ cup grated Parmesan cheese
1 tablespoon coarse salt
Salt and pepper to taste.

Cook's Tip

You can use a 28-ounce can of plum tomatoes in puree instead of fresh tomatoes. Mash the tomatoes with a fork.

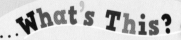

What's This?

Basil is an herb with large, deep-green leaves. It is best to tear delicate basil leaves with your fingers instead of using a knife.

Let's Cook!

1. Fill a large pot halfway with hot water. Place over high heat on the stove.

1. Wash, peel, and chop tomatoes. Throw away the seeds.

2. In a frying pan, heat oil and sauté onion and garlic for about 5 minutes. Add tomatoes, basil leaves, salt, and pepper. Simmer for 20 minutes, stirring often.

3. When water in the large pot is boiling, add coarse salt and spaghetti. Cook for the amount of time shown on the package. Stir often so pasta doesn't stick. Drain spaghetti in a colander and place in a serving dish.

4. Spoon tomato sauce over spaghetti and stir gently until the sauce is spread evenly over the spaghetti. Add Parmesan cheese. Serve warm in bowls with a basil leaf on top.

Makes 6–8 servings.

Cook's Tip

Pasta should be cooked al dente (**all DEN-tay**); this means it should be chewy, not mushy. Break open a piece of cooked pasta. If you see a thin white line or white dots in the middle, it's not done yet. The inside of the pasta should all be clear yellow.

Chapter 5

Wiener Schnitzel

Wiener schnitzel (*VEE-nur shnit-sel*) is a special dish from Austria. Thin slices of veal are breaded and then deeped-fried. There is a story that hundreds of years ago, the ruler of Austria liked his veal covered in flakes of gold. People wanted to eat what he ate, but most could not afford to wrap their food in gold. A golden breadcrumb covering was created instead.

Austria

Austria is located in the middle of Europe, next to Germany. Wiener schitznel comes from Vienna, the capital city (called "Wien" in Austria). Vienna was the home of many famous musicians and composers, such as Beethoven, Mozart, and Haydn.

What You Need

Equipment:
Meat mallet or rolling pin
Three bowls
Large skillet
Tongs
plastic wrap
gallon-size plastic bag
paper towels

Ingredients:
Vegetable oil for frying
4 veal cutlets
¼ cup all-purpose flour
¼ teaspoon salt
2 eggs, lightly beaten
1 cup dry plain breadcrumbs
1 lemon

What's This?

A meat mallet is a two-sided kitchen hammer used to flatten boneless meat.

Let's Cook!

1. Wrap the veal cutlets with plastic wrap or put in a 1 gallon plastic bag. Flatten the cutlets with a meat mallet or a rolling pin until they are only 1/4-inch thick. Remove the plastic wrap.

2. Combine the flour and salt in one bowl. Beat the eggs in a second bowl. Put the breadcrumbs in a third bowl.

3. Heat ¼ inch oil in a large skillet on the stove on medium heat.

4. First dip a veal cutlet in the flour mixture. Then dip it in the egg, shaking off the extra. Finally, lightly dip it in the breadcrumbs and, with an adult's help, place it in the skillet. Repeat for all the cutlets.

5. Cook the veal for four minutes on each side until golden brown. Use tongs to flip the cutlets and remove them when done. Drain cutlets on a paper towel.

6. Serve warm right away, so breading doesn't get soggy.Cut the lemon in half. Add a squirt of lemon juice on top.

Makes 4 servings.

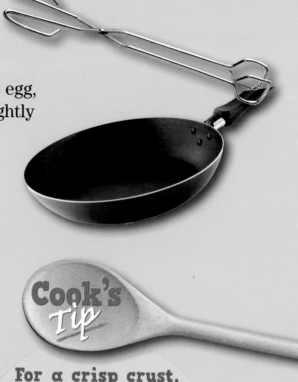

Cook's Tip

For a crisp crust, make sure the cutlet is fried in enough oil so it "swims."

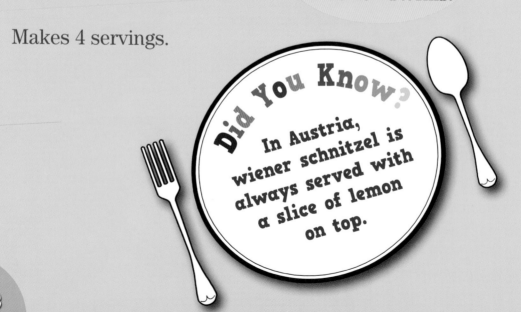

Did You Know?

In Austria, wiener schnitzel is always served with a slice of lemon on top.

Chapter 6

Tacos de Pescado
(Fish Tacos)

A taco is a traditional Mexican dish. A tortilla is wrapped or folded around a filling, and salsa and cheese are added on top. This version, tacos de pescado (*TAH-cos day pess-CAH-doe*), is popular in Mexican coastal fishing villages.

Mexico

Mexico is in North America, south of the United States. Corn is grown all over Mexico. It is ground up and made into a tortilla, which is a very flat bread. Tortilla comes from the Spanish word "torta," which means "round cake." Tortillas come in different colors depending on the type of corn that is used.

What You Need

Equipment:

Baking sheet
Parchment paper
Medium mixing bowl
Plate

Ingredients:

1 pound boneless
fresh fish, (use a firm white
fish such as tilapia, snapper,
or cod), cut into large chunks

½ cup cornmeal

½ teaspoon salt

½ teaspoon pepper

½ teaspoon cumin

¼ teaspoon chili powder
(only use if you like spicy
food)

2 eggs, lightly beaten

2 limes

4–8 corn tortillas
or taco shells

Salsa (or you can use
tartar sauce)

Shredded taco cheese

Shredded lettuce

What's This?

Salsa is a sauce of
tomatoes, onions, and
chili peppers used on top
of tacos. It is sold in jars
in the market in either
the Mexican food or
chips aisle.

Let's Cook!

1. Preheat oven to 400°F (204°C).

2. Line a cookie sheet with parchment paper or grease lightly with vegetable oil.

3. In a medium bowl, combine beaten eggs, salt, pepper, and cumin.

4. Pour cornmeal on a small plate. If you like spicy food, mix in chili powder.

5. Dip each chunk of fish in the egg mixture and then coat it with the cornmeal (dip it into the cornmeal so that the cornmeal sticks to the fish). Place on the baking sheet. Repeat with all pieces of fish.

6. Bake fish in oven for 20 minutes. Have an adult help turn over the fish halfway through. Remove fish from the oven using oven mitts. Cut lime in half. Squeeze lime juice over the fish.

7. To make the tacos, place about two chunks of cooked fish on a tortilla or inside a taco shell. Top with shredded lettuce, salsa, and shredded cheese.

Makes 4–6 servings.

Cook's Tip

Tortillas need to be warmed in an oven or a microwave before folding around the taco filling or they will crack and everything will spill out.

Did You Know?

Tacos are supposed to be eaten with your hands.

Chapter 7

Papaya Chicken and Coconut Milk

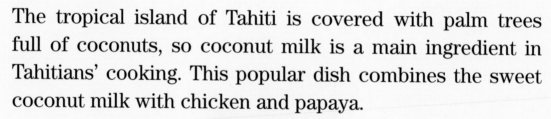

The tropical island of Tahiti is covered with palm trees full of coconuts, so coconut milk is a main ingredient in Tahitians' cooking. This popular dish combines the sweet coconut milk with chicken and papaya.

Tahiti

There are thousands of islands in the South Pacific Ocean. Tahiti is part of a group of islands, or archipelago (*are-kih-PEL-uh-go*), called Polynesia. It is the largest island in French Polynesia.

What You Need

Equipment:
Cutting board
Sharp knife
Large frying pan
Small saucepan

Ingredients:
4 boneless, skinless
chicken breasts, cut into
cubes
1 ripe papaya
1¾ cups coconut milk
1 onion, chopped
3 tablespoons olive oil
Salt and pepper to taste

Cook's Tip

You can use frozen
papaya chunks
instead of fresh
papaya.

What's This?

Coconut milk is not
the liquid inside a
coconut. The "milk"
comes from pressing
the inner white flesh
of the fruit.

1. Peel the papaya, remove the seeds, and cut into thin slices or chunks.

2. In a large frying pan, with an adult's help, heat the olive oil. Cook the chicken cubes over high heat until the chicken is cooked throughly. Add chopped onions and cook for 5 more minutes. Add sliced papaya, salt, and pepper. Cook for another 5 minutes. Remove chicken mixture from stove.

3. In a small saucepan, heat coconut milk until warm. Pour over chicken mixture and serve over white rice.

Makes 4 servings.

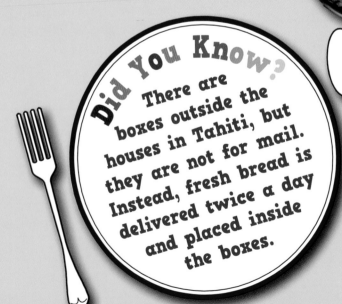

Did You Know?

There are boxes outside the houses in Tahiti, but they are not for mail. Instead, fresh bread is delivered twice a day and placed inside the boxes.

Chapter 8

Shepherd's Pie

Shepherd's pie is a British meat pie with mashed potatoes. There is no crust to the pie. Instead, a layer of ground meat and a few vegetables are topped with creamy mashed potatoes.

United Kingdom

In northern England and Scotland, shepherd's pie is also known as "cottage pie." This area of the United Kingdom has many sheep herds. A shepherd moves the sheep from place to place. Shepherd's pie was a favorite hearty dish enjoyed by shepherds after a long day in the fields.

35

What You Need

Equipment:
Large pot
Colander
Potato masher
Large frying pan
Cutting board
Knife
Large mixing bowl
Large baking dish
Fork

Ingredients:
3 large potatoes, peeled and cubed
2 teaspoons salt
6 tablespoons butter
½ cup sour cream
1 large onion, minced
1 large carrot, chopped
1 pound ground beef or ground lamb
1 clove garlic, minced
½ teaspoon thyme
1 teaspoon Worcestershire (*WUSS-ta-sheer*) sauce
½ cup beef broth
¼ teaspoon pepper
Salt

Cook's Tip

To make this dish faster and easier to prepare, use leftover ground meat or instant mashed potatoes. You can also add corn, peas, or celery to the meat mixture.

Let's Cook!

1. Boil potatoes in a large pot of salted water on the stove for 15–20 minutes, until tender.

2. While potatoes cook, melt 2 tablespoons of butter in a large frying pan. Sauté onion for about 10 minutes and then add carrot. Add ground beef and cook until meat is no longer pink.

3. Add garlic, thyme, Worcestershire sauce, pepper, and beef broth.

4. Ask an adult to help you remove the potatoes from the stove. Drain in a colander and then place in a large mixing bowl. Add 4 tablespoons of butter, sour cream, and a dash of salt and pepper. Mash potatoes until creamy.

5. Preheat oven to 400°F (204°C). Spread beef mixture in a buttered baking dish. Evenly spread mashed potatoes on top of the beef. Use a fork to make small peaks in the potatoes. Bake in oven for 25 minutes and place under broiler for 5 minutes, or until top is lightly browned.

6. Remove from oven. Cool for 5 minutes and serve.

Makes 4 servings.

What's This?

You can mash potatoes using a potato masher, a heavy fork, or an electric mixer. A potato masher lets you push down on the soft, cooked potato and mash it easily.

Chapter 9

Psari Spetsiotiko

(Baked Fish With Tomatoes and Bread Crumbs)

Psari Spetsiotiko (*PSAH-dee speh-tzhee-OH-tee-koh*) is baked fish topped with chopped tomatoes and bread crumbs. It comes from a small island in Greece called Spetses, which is near Athens, the country's capital.

Greece

Greece is a country in the southeast of Europe. It is on the southern tip of the Balkan peninsula. Fishing is popular in Greece, so people there eat a lot of fish. The fish is fresh and cooked simply.

What You Need

Equipment:
Glass baking dish
Medium mixing bowl
Large spoon
Paring knife
Juicer

Ingredients:
2 pounds red snapper, halibut, or cod
Juice of 1 lemon
1½ cups diced canned tomatoes or 4 cups fresh tomatoes, chopped
4 cloves garlic, minced
½ cup fresh parsley, minced
½ cup bread crumbs
Olive oil

Cook's Tip

Wash and store parsley in a damp paper towel in the refrigerator.

Let's Cook!

1. Preheat oven to 350°F (180°C).

2. In a medium mixing bowl, combine chopped tomatoes, garlic, and parsley. Let sit for 15 minutes, but not in the refrigerator.

3. Place fish in one layer in a glass baking dish. Cover fish with lemon juice.

4. Spoon tomato mixture evenly on top of the fish. Then sprinkle the bread crumbs on top of the tomatoes. Drizzle olive oil over the bread crumbs.

5. Bake in the oven for 30–35 minutes. Halfway through, have an adult open the oven and use a large spoon to baste the fish with the liquid in the pan.

6. Remove from the oven with oven mitts and serve hot.

Makes 4–6 servings.

What's This?

To baste means to pour liquid over fish or meat while it is cooking, so it stays moist.

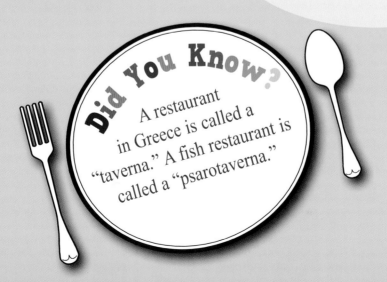

Did You Know?

A restaurant in Greece is called a "taverna." A fish restaurant is called a "psarotaverna."

Chapter 10

Beef or Chicken Satay

In Thailand, satay (*sah-TAY*) is spiced meat or chicken served on a stick—which makes it fun and easy to eat. This shish kebab–style meal is often dipped in a creamy peanut sauce.

Thailand

Thailand is in southeast Asia. Food stalls line the streets of the capital city of Bangkok, and satay is sold at many of them. Chefs in Thailand cook so every meal combines the five main tastes: salty, sweet, sour, bitter, and spicy.

What You Need

Equipment:

Medium mixing bowl
Glass baking dish
Plastic wrap
Aluminum foil
Blender
Small bowl
Paring knife
Juicer
Bamboo skewers

What's This?

Bamboo skewers are thin wooden sticks used to hold food while grilling or roasting. They can be found in your market.

Ingredients:

1 pound beef tenderloin or boneless, skinless chicken breasts, cut into long strips

For marinade:

2 tablespoons soy sauce
¼ cup orange juice
2 tablespoons peanut oil
1 teaspoon minced garlic
1 tablespoon curry powder
½ teaspoon ground coriander
¼ teaspoon crushed red pepper flakes

For dipping sauce:

½ up peanut butter
2 tablespoons sesame oil
¼ cup onion, minced
1 clove garlic, minced
Juice of 1 lime
2 tablespoons brown sugar
½ cup boiling water

Let's Cook!

1. In a medium mixing bowl, combine all the marinade ingredients.

2. Place the beef or chicken strips in a glass baking dish. Pour the marinade over the meat to coat it. Cover dish with plastic wrap or aluminum foil and place in refrigerator for 2 hours. Occasionally shake the pan to keep meat covered.

3. Line a baking pan with foil. Preheat oven to broil.

4. Thread the beef or chicken strips onto the wet bamboo sticks and place on baking sheet. Place sheet in oven and broil for 6 minutes until cooked through.

5. Combine all the dipping sauce ingredients in a blender and blend for 30 seconds. Add more hot water if sauce is too thick. Spoon sauce into a bowl and serve with satay.

Makes 4–6 servings.

Cook's Tip

It is important to soak the wooden skewers in water for at least 30 minutes—otherwise the wooden sticks will burn in the oven.

Did You Know?

The word satay means "triple stacked," and most satays in Thailand have three strips or cubes of meat.

43

Chapter 11

Quiche Lorraine

Quiche (*keesh*) tastes almost like a scrambled-egg pie. This dish comes from France, which is in Europe. Different regions of the country bake different ingredients inside their quiche, such as vegetables, seafood, and meats.

France

Quiche Lorraine (*loh-RAIN*), made with bacon and cheese, is the most popular kind of quiche. This kind comes from the northeastern part of France. More than 350 kinds of cheese are made there.

What You Need

Equipment:
Baking sheet
Medium bowl
Whisk

Ingredients:
1 9-inch frozen prepared pie crust, unbaked

5 bacon slices, cooked and cut into small pieces

1 ¼ cups shredded Swiss cheese

4 large eggs

1 cup milk

½ cup heavy cream

¼ teaspoon salt

¼ teaspoon black pepper

⅛ teaspoon nutmeg

What's This?

Baking pie crust from scratch takes a lot of time. Find ready-made pie crust in the freezer aisle in your market.

Cook's Tip

An easy way to cut cooked bacon into small pieces is with clean kitchen scissors.

Let's Cook!

1. Place pie crust in pan on a baking sheet. Poke a few holes with a fork on the bottom and sides of the pie crust so the crust does not become uneven while baking.

2. Preheat oven to 375°F (190°C).

3. Sprinkle chopped bacon and shredded cheese over the bottom of the pie crust.

4. In a medium bowl, beat eggs, milk, and cream with a whisk. Add salt, pepper, and nutmeg. Pour mixture over bacon and cheese in pie crust.

5. Bake in the middle of the oven for 35 minutes or until a knife inserted in the center of the quiche comes out clean. Remove with oven mitts.

6. Cool quiche for 10 minutes and then slice into wedges. Serve.

Makes 6–8 servings.

Did You Know?

Quiche was invented in the 16th century to celebrate the arrival of spring.

Further Reading

Books

D'Amico, Joan, and Karen Eich Drummond. *The Coming to America Cookbook: Delicious Recipes and Fascinating Stories From America's Many Cultures.* Hoboken, N.J.: John Wiley, & Sons,, Inc. 2005.

De Mariaffi, Elisabeth. *Eat It Up! Lip-Smacking Recipes for Kids.* Toronto, Canada: Owlkids, 2009.

Dodge, Abigail Johnson. *Around the World Cookbook.* New York: DK Publishing, 2008.

Lagasse, Emeril. *Emeril's There's a Chef in My World!: Recipes That Take You Places.* New York: HarperCollins Publishers, 2006.

Locricchio, Matthew. *The 2nd International Cookbook for Kids.* New York : Marshall Cavendish, 2008.

Wagner, Lisa. *Cool Sweets & Treats to Eat: Easy Recipes for Kids to Cook.* Edina, Minn.: ABDO Publishing Co., 2007.

Internet Addresses

Cookalotamus Kids
<http://www.cookalotamus.com/kids.html>

PBS Kids: Cafe Zoom
<http://pbskids.org/zoom/activities/cafe/>

Spatulatta.com
<http://www.spatulatta.com/>

Index